CONTENTMENT

Healing the hunger
of our hearts
by Anne Woodcock

Series Editor: Tim Chester

Contentment: healing the hunger of our hearts
© Anne Woodcock/The Good Book Company, 2008

The Good Book Company
Tel: 0845-225-0880
Fax: 0845-225-0990
Email: admin@thegoodbook.co.uk
Internet: www.thegoodbook.co.uk

ISBN 13: 9781905564668

Printed in China

Contents

Introduction: Good Book Guides

Every Bible-study group is different—yours may take place in a church building, in a home, in a cafe, on a train, over a leisurely mid-morning coffee or squashed into a 30-minute lunch break. Your group may include new Christians, mature Christians, non-Christians, students, business colleagues or teens. That's why we've designed these *Good Book Guides* to be flexible for use in many different situations.

Our aim in each session is to uncover the meaning of a passage, and see how it fits into the 'big picture' of the Bible. But that can never be the end. We also need to apply appropriately what we have discovered to our lives. Let's take a look at what is included:

⬌ **Talkabout:** most groups need to 'break the ice' at the beginning of a session, and here's the question that will do that. It's designed to get people talking around a subject that will be covered in the course of the Bible study.

⬇ **Investigate:** the Bible text for each session is broken up into manageable chunks, with questions that aim to help you understand what the passage is about. **The Leader's Guide** contains **guidance on questions**, and sometimes ⌄ additional 'follow-up' questions.

⌣ **Explore more (optional):** these questions will help you connect what you have learned to other parts of the Bible, so you can begin to understand how the Bible relates together as a whole.

➔ **Apply:** As you go through a Bible study, you'll keep coming across **apply** sections. Some of these have questions to get the group discussing what the Bible teaching means in practice for you and your church. Sometimes, a ⌣ **getting personal** section is an opportunity for you to think, plan and pray about the changes that you personally may need to make as a result of what you have discovered.

⬆ **Pray:** We want to encourage prayer that is rooted in God's word—in line with His concerns, purposes and promises. So each session ends with an opportunity to review the truths and challenges highlighted by the Bible study, and turn them into prayers of request and thanksgiving.

The **Leader's Guide** and introduction provide historical background information, explanations of the Bible texts for each session, ideas for **optional extra** activities, and guidance on how best to help people uncover the truths of God's word.

Why study *Contentment*?

We live in a society that thrives on discontent. Through a multitude of different ways—advertising, celebrity gossip, makeover shows—people make money out of other people's discontent. It's no surprise then that we all know what it is to lack contentment in our lives—with what we have, how much we can get, what we do, who we live with, what we are like and what the future promises.

The constant hunger for something more may seem like the aches and pains of growing old—something that we must just put up with in this far-from-perfect world. It is true, as these Bible studies will show, that life without God will never satisfy. But the Bible also shows that discontent is the symptom of a lethal disease that will kill us if we do not find a cure. It was discontent that first led humans into rebellion against God, with the catastrophic consequences that have followed from that decision.

Even when we come to know God as our loving Father through Jesus Christ, one of the Christian's greatest struggles is fighting the temptation to be discontent. The stakes are high—a discontent Christian will become a negative influence on other Christians, a poor witness for the Lord Jesus Christ, depressed and resentful towards God and distracted from the gospel. Ultimately, discontent in the church leads to false teaching and loss of faith.

Yet Jesus Christ promises that anyone who believes in Him will never again hunger or thirst. The apostle Paul was able to say that he had learned the secret of being content in any and every situation—in need or in plenty. Discontent is a problem of our hearts, not our circumstances. This Good Book Guide can help us to understand why we become discontented, how Jesus Christ alone can help us, and on a practical level, how Christian living can bring the treasure of contentment to our daily lives.

Ecclesiastes
OUR HUNGRY HEARTS

⊕ talkabout

1. Can you remember a time when you felt blissfully contented, even for just a few moments? What put an end to it?

⊻ investigate

Ecclesiastes was written by a king of Israel, who called himself 'the Teacher'. He seems to have been powerful and prosperous, and to have ruled during a period of peace and stability. He wrote this book 'to study and to explore by wisdom all that is done under heaven' (1 v 13).

> **▶ Read Ecclesiastes 1 v 1-14**

2. How does the Teacher feel about life? (See for example v 2, 8, and 14.)

• Do you find this surprising? Why?

3. Look at the following verses from Ecclesiastes. In the Teacher's search for meaning and contentment, what did he try, and what did he discover?

What did he try out?	What did he discover?
1 v 16-18; 2 v 12-16	1 v 18
	2 v 16
2 v 1-3	v 11
2 v 4-6	
2 v 7-8	
2 v 9	
2 v 17-23	v 18-19
	v 23

⮊ apply

4. Look at the list of things that the Teacher turned to in order to find meaning and fulfilment. Where do you see this same search in the lives of people around us? And the same disappointment?

Which of these things are you depending on for a happy and fulfilled life? Or is there something else that you look to? Most of these things—relationships, family, work, leisure, achievements, experiences—can be good and enjoyable. But what is the Teacher's warning to us?

⊍ **investigate**

▶ **Read Ecclesiastes 2 v 24-25.**

5. The Teacher realises that not everyone feels the same way as he does. Some people are quite content, perhaps because they keep busy and don't think about the meaning of life. But what does the Teacher want these people to understand?

▶ **Read Ecclesiastes 9 v 1-12**

6. In these verses he mentions the one great problem for us that makes everything 'under the sun' meaningless. What is that problem?

7. In view of this, what is the best that we can hope for in this life? (See 9 v 7-10 and also 11 v 7-9.)

▶ Read the following verses from Ecclesiastes:

'I devoted myself to study and to explore by wisdom all that is done under heaven. What a heavy burden God has laid on men!' **1 v 13**

'I have seen the burden God has laid on men. He has made everything beautiful in its time. He has also set eternity in the hearts of men; yet they cannot fathom what God has done from beginning to end.' **3 v 10-11**

8. What is God's part in the discontent and despair that the Teacher discovers as he investigates life?

➔ apply

9. Why do you think God has done this?

⊡ explore more

optional

In Romans 1 the apostle Paul gives us a summary of the causes and results of human rebellion against God, that first occurred at the beginning of history in the Garden of Eden. **Read Romans 1 v 18-25.**

According to these verses...

- *What do people know about God? (v 20)*

- *How do they know this? (v 20)*

- *How should people respond to God? (v 21)*

- *How do people respond to God? (v 18, 21, 23)*

- *Why do they respond to God in this way? (v 18, 24)*

- *What is the result of this human rebellion against God? (v 18, v 21-22, v 24-25)*

How can this passage help us understand why God has laid on humans the burden of dissatisfaction with life 'under the sun'?

⬇ investigate

❯ Read Ecclesiastes 12 v 1, 6-7, 13-14

10. What is the Teacher's conclusion?

* When should we put this into practice? (See v 1, 6-7.)

➡ apply

11. What has the Teacher's investigation shown us about our search for contentment?

⊡ getting personal

What do you do when you are discontented? Do you go from one thing to another in a search for fulfilment? Can you now understand how God might use your dissatisfaction to turn you back to Himself?

Or perhaps you are really enjoying life right now. Have you realised that your good gifts come from God, and these should lead you to a life of thanking and glorifying Him? Do you understand that without God, life is ultimately meaningless?

⏏ **pray**

- Think of someone (a person you know or someone in the news) who is struggling with despair at the meaninglessness of life. Let your prayers for that person be shaped by what you have learned this session.

- Think about how the book of Ecclesiastes can be used to reach the people of today. Pray that you, your church and your leaders can use these truths to help people turn to God.

John 6 v 25-42; 60-69

THE ONLY FOOD THAT SATISFIES

⊕ talkabout

1. Many people—even those who are not 'religious'—will instinctively pray at certain times in their lives. In your experience, when do people turn to prayer, and what kind of things do they pray about at these times?

⊕ investigate

The Bible passage in this session comes just after Jesus had miraculously fed 5,000 people on the shores of Lake Galilee (John 6 v 1-13). Many of those who had seen this miracle now came looking for Him.

▶ Read John 6 v 25-42

2. What do these people want from Jesus (v 26, 30-31)?

3. What does Jesus want them to have (v 27)?

- What does He think of their ambitions?

4. Jesus tells us to work for 'food that endures to eternal life'. How can we get this 'food'? (v 27-29)?

- What does this tell us about Jesus?

Jesus' miracles aren't party tricks—they are *signs*, pointing to who He really is. Jesus wants people to come to Him in a way that shows they understand who He really is.

5. What, in fact, do these people really think of Jesus?

- v 14-15:

- v 30-31:

- v 41-42:

- How would they have responded differently if they had been looking for Him because of what the miraculous signs showed Him to be?

⊡ apply

6. Many people (even some who claim to be Christians) still misunderstand Jesus and end up working for 'food that spoils'.
Can you think of ways in which this happens today?

- What *should* we be seeking from Jesus? (What should we be asking Him for?)

⊡ getting personal

Are you tempted to treat God like this—as someone who is only there to give you happiness, health or prosperity here and now?
Why is this so wrong?

⊡ investigate

7. Jesus doesn't only promise to give eternal life (v 27); He says that He *is* the bread of life (v 35). What does that mean?

8. What does Jesus mean when He says: 'He who comes to me will never go hungry, and he who believes in me will never be thirsty' (v 35)?

• How can this help us when we become discontent?

⊡ explore more

optional

Jesus made a very similar promise just two chapters previously in John's Gospel. **Read John 4 v 4-19 and 25-29.** Look at the similarities:
- *What does Jesus offer this woman (v 10, 14)?*

- *How can we get what Jesus offers (v 10, 14)?*

- *At the beginning of the story, how is the woman similar to the crowd in John 6 (v 11-12)?*

- *At the end of the story, how does the woman respond to Jesus (see v 28-29)?*

Look at the extra insights that this story gives us:
- *Jesus makes His offer to a sinful, Samaritan woman. Look at verses 9, 17-18 and 27. What does that tell us about His promise?*

- *Look at verse 14. How can we expect to be changed by what Jesus offers?*

⊡ investigate

❯ **Read John 6 v 60-69**

9. Why do you think that 'many of his disciples' responded to Jesus' promise of eternal life by leaving Him? (See v 14-15, 26, 41-42, 57, 65).

10. What did Simon Peter and the Twelve understand that the other 'disciples' did not (see v 68-69)?

• How can we get this kind of understanding (see v 65)?

(see v 65)

⊡ apply

11. What should be our first response to discontent—in ourselves or in others?

• What are our chances of finding contentment in this world?

12. How have you found Jesus brings satisfaction? Think about the difference Christ has brought to the way you view life, and share your experience with the group, for their encouragement

⊡ getting personal

Have you come to Jesus and believed in Him? Has it been your experience that your 'core emptiness' has been filled? Do you understand what it is to daily feed on Jesus, the bread of life—is Jesus that vital to you?

⊞ pray

- Thank God that there is a remedy for the meaninglessness of life in our fallen world—Jesus, the bread of God, who gives life to the world. Thank God for the promise that whoever comes to Jesus will never go hungry.

- Confess those times when you have been working for food that spoils, when you have grumbled because Jesus doesn't fit your agenda, or when you have doubted or despised His promise to give eternal life.

- Pray for yourself and others struggling with discontent, that your first response would be to turn to Jesus.

3

1 Timothy 6 v 3-19

CONTENT WITH WHAT WE HAVE

⬌ talkabout

1. What do people find enjoyable about new or favourite possessions? Would you find them so enjoyable if you lived on a desert island?

Everyone suffers from pain, difficulty and frustration because the world has been spoiled by our rebellion against God. But Jesus said: 'He who comes to me will never go hungry, and he who believes in me will never be thirsty'. So how can it be possible for a Christian to be satisfied and content, while still living in this spoiled world?

⬇ investigate

❯ Read 1 Timothy 6 v 3-10

2. Paul is concerned about false teachers. In v 3-5 what do we learn about:
• their fruit (the things they do)?

• their character?

• what drives them?

3. If you could choose a key characteristic that shows the difference between a man of God and a false teacher, what would it be?

• Now look at verse 6. What characteristic does Paul highlight? Why do you think he chooses that one?

4. In verse 9 Paul describes the desire to get rich as a 'trap'. What lies behind this desire and what will happen to us if we pursue riches (v 9-10)?

⤷ **apply**

5. 'The love of money is a root of all kinds of evil' (v 10). People find it easy to agree with this statement and to point out where other people go wrong. But how can we disguise the love of money in our own lives, and dress it up to look like something good?

Contentment: healing the hunger of our hearts

⊡ getting personal

Do you disguise your love of money as something good? Are you flirting with 'foolish and harmful desires'? For example, how much time do you spend time on TV programmes or magazines that make you envy others? Does your standard of living get you down? Do you dream about winning the lottery?

If any of this is true of you, do you realise how serious the problem is? Where could you end up? Take action now!

⊡ investigate

According to Paul, 'godliness with contentment' is the true treasure that makes us wealthy (v 6). When we live in this way, we are not under any delusions—we have a true understanding of our situation and of what is important in life.

6. According to Paul, what is the truth about...

- our right to own things (v 7)?

- our future (v 7)?

- our needs (v 8)?

- What will a true understanding of these things save us from?

▶ Read 1 Timothy 6 v 11-19

Paul turns his attention to Christians and church leaders—the 'man of God' (v 11), and those under his care (v 17-19). He answers the question 'What will help us to escape the devil's trap?'

7. What are Paul's instructions for the man of God (v 11-12)? Find four things that Paul tells Timothy to do, and discuss what each means.

- v 11: _____

- v 11: _____

- v 12: _____

- v 12: _____

8. What will keep the man of God on the right track (v 13-16)? Find four encouragements in these verses, and discuss how they could help you to resist the temptation to pursue riches.

- v 13: _____

- v 13: _____

- v 14: _____

- v 15-16: _____

9. We may think that it is easier to be content when we are rich, but for Paul, wealth brings its own serious problems. What are they (v 17)?

10. What is the antidote to being led astray by financial wealth (v 18-19)?

➔ apply

11. Anyone who lives in the west is rich beyond the dreams of most of the world's population, so Paul's warning in v 17 will be very relevant to all of us. In what ways can the western church show arrogance, and put hope in wealth rather than God?

• How can we put into practice the antidote that Paul outlines in v 18-19? Be as practical as possible in your suggestions.

12. Most people today think that more wealth will bring more contentment. What have you learned that should change that view?

⊡ getting personal

Would you describe yourself as someone who is rich in good deeds? What can you do to become more generous and willing to share? Think of one thing that you could start doing right now, and make a commitment to do it.

⊞ explore more

The New Testament writer, James, concerned about rich people who claim to be Christians, gives us a description of covetous (greedy and envious) people in **James 4 v 1-10.**

- *What causes the problem—people's personal circumstances or something else (v 1)?*

- *What has happened to these people's relationship with God (v 2-3)?*

- *Where do they end up in their relationship with God (v 4)?*

- *Look at James' antidote to this 'spiritual adultery' (v 7-10). How does this tie in with Paul's words to Timothy?*

- *What additional insight does James give us in these verses?*

Here is another New Testament writer pointing out the eternal danger of giving in to discontent and pursuing worldly riches!

- *What action will you take to deal with discontent (now or in the future) in this area of your life?*

⬆ **pray**

- Reflect on what you have learned about the dangers of wealth, and the final destiny of all those who love money.

- Pray for mercy and forgiveness, for yourself and others who are caught in this trap of the devil.

4

1 Corinthians 7 v 1-24

CONTENT WITH WHERE WE ARE

⊕ talkabout

1. Share ways in which people today live by the saying: 'A change does you good'. Why do we believe that?

⊕ investigate

This session looks at how a Christian should respond in a situation (eg: marriage, singleness, job) that seems far from ideal. 1 Corinthians is written to a church facing many issues for the first time. Someone had asked Paul for guidance, particularly on singleness and marriage.

> **Read 1 Corinthians 7 v 1-16**

2. What are the questions posed by the Corinthians that Paul is answering? Match the issues with the verses.

a. v 1-2, 8-9	**1.** An unbeliever decides to leave their marriage to a Christian: *should the Christian fight to preserve the marriage or not?*
b. v 3-7	**2.** Christians who are married: *should they separate/divorce or not?*
c. v 10-11	**3.** Christians who are married: *should they have sex or not?*
d. v 12-14	**4.** Christians who are unmarried or widows: *should they get married or not?*
e. v 15-16	**5.** A Christian married to an unbeliever who is happy with the marriage: *should the Christian divorce or not?*

3. For Paul, what is most important when deciding what to do? Go through the situations again and complete the table below to identify Paul's priorities.

Situation	Verse	Paul's priority
a. (v 1-2, 8-9)	v 1 (Find Paul's reasons for this in v 32, 38, 40)	
	v 9	
b. (v 3-7)	v 5b	
c. (v 10-11)	v 10-11 (See also v 19b.)	
d. (v 12-14) **e.** (v 15-16)	v 16	

Paul has **four priorities** that determine how Christians should act:
- Devotion to the Lord's affairs
- Protection from Satan's temptations
- Obedience to the Lord's commands
- Bringing unbelievers to Christ

> **Read 1 Corinthians 7 v 17-24**

4. What is the **key principle** for the whole passage that Paul gives us here (v 17, 20, 24)?

5. What are the reasons behind this principle?
Write down Paul's argument given in each verse

- v 17: _____

- v 19: _____

- v 21-23: _____

- v 24: _____

Contentment: healing the hunger of our hearts

⊕ apply

6. Look at how the experience of being a slave is transformed when someone becomes a Christian (v 22). What low-status situations in our society can also be transformed by the truth of the Christian message?

7. Look again at Paul's four reasons for the principle that 'each one should remain in the situation which he was in when God called him' (Q5). How can we help one another to be guided by these truths, rather than the values of the world (be as practical as possible)?

⊡ getting personal

Which of Paul's priorities (Q3) do you share, and which do you need to take on board? Have you reached the point where you are willing to sacrifice your own ambitions for the sake of these things?

⊡ explore more

optional

❯ Read 2 Kings 5 v 1-3, 9-15.

One of God's people, an Israelite girl, is in a very un-ideal situation. Yet her faithfulness to God in that situation brings great glory to His name.

- *What was difficult and unpleasant about the young girl's situation?*

- *How might you have been tempted to react in this situation?*

- *How did the young girl show faith in God, and why was this remarkable in the circumstances?*

- *How does the story of this young girl demonstrate the wisdom of Paul's words to Christians in un-ideal situations?*

⊌ investigate

8. How can we see that Paul is not always against people improving their situation in life (v 21)?

⊕ apply

9. Look again at Paul's four priorities.
- Devotion to the Lord's affairs
- Protection from Satan's temptations
- Obedience to the Lord's commands
- Bringing unbelievers to Christ

How could these four priorities help us to give good biblical advice in the following situations?

1. Max is a Christian who lives, works and goes to church in the same town. His job is secure and close to home, bringing in an average salary and taking up 40-45 hours a week, but it's dull and not really how he imagines spending the rest of his life. At church he is beginning to get involved in youth work, and is starting to think about becoming a ministry apprentice. His uncle, a successful entrepreneur in the city, but not a believer, wants Max to work for him, with a view to ultimately taking over management of one of his companies. This is a unique opportunity, promising not only high-quality training, and access to influential people, but also a substantial salary. However, Max would have to move away to London. What advice would you give to him about this job offer?

2. Kellie is a teenage mother. She became pregnant at 16 by Joe, her boyfriend of three years. At ante-natal classes she met a Christian woman who told her about Jesus. Kellie decided to become a Christian herself. Joe is not a Christian but he wants to stay with Kellie and the baby, and is willing to get married if that is what Kellie would like. Kellie is really keen to grow in her faith, and she dreams of her baby growing up in a Christian family, but Joe, although he is very good to Kellie, shows no interest at all in the Christian faith. Kellie wonders whether she should split up with Joe, so that if a Christian man comes her way she would be free to marry him. How would you advise Kellie about this relationship?

10. Look again at the four reasons for Paul's key principle (see question 5):
- God has called each of us to our present situation, so He has a purpose for us there.
- What is important to God is keeping His commands, rather than trying to improve our situation.
- Our situation is transformed by the fact that we are now Christians.
- We are responsible to God in the decisions we make about our situation—we don't have to fit in with what other people expect.

How will these four truths encourage Max and Kellie in their difficult situations?

☺ getting personal

Could you give a fellow Christian, not just tea and sympathy, but solid biblical advice, like Paul's? Do you know the Bible well enough to advise and encourage Christians struggling in un-ideal situations? Are you willing to speak out, even when the Bible's guidance is difficult to accept?

⬆ pray

- **On your own:** Pray for yourself (or for someone you know) in an un-ideal situation. Pray for God to open your eyes to His purposes, which He is working out in that very situation. Pray that you will see things as God sees them and that your view of this difficult situation will be transformed.

- **Together:** Thank God for each other and pray that you would grow together in helping one another in every situation to live as God's people, devoted to His work, obeying His commands, resisting temptation and witnessing to others.

5

2 Corinthians 1 and 4

CONTENT WHEN LIFE IS HARD

⊕ talkabout

1. When something goes wrong, what's the first thing you are likely to do? What do these responses show about our relationship with God?

2 Corinthians is a deeply personal letter from Paul, in which he makes public his love, longings, distress, and sufferings for the church.

⊕ investigate

> ▶ **Read 2 Corinthians 1 v 1-11**

2. According to Paul, why will troubles be unavoidable for Christians (v 5)?

3. What kind of things did Christ suffer, and so what kind of things should His followers expect to suffer?

4. What can Christians be confident of when they experience troubles (v 3-4)?

5. What good does Paul expect to come out of Christian suffering?

- v 6: _____

- v 9: _____

- v 11: _____

- How can this help us to find contentment when life is hard?

⊡ apply

6. Can you think of any examples—from the Bible, from history, or from your own experience—of the way in which great good has come from the sufferings of Christians?

⊡ getting personal

What are you most frightened of happening in your life? Do you believe that God can and will comfort you even in this, your worst fear?

⊡ investigate

> **❯ Read 2 Corinthians 4 v 7-18**

7. What does Paul mean when he says that we have the treasure of the good news about Jesus 'in jars of clay' (v 7)?

8. Why has God chosen this way to show Jesus Christ to the world?

⊟ apply

9. Paul talks about God's all-surpassing power (v 7) and Jesus' life (v 11) being put on display in our weak and dying bodies. How might this work in practice? Think of some examples.

⊡ investigate

10. What is the hope that keeps Paul going (v 13-18)?

- How does he describe his troubles in the light of this hope?

- What does it mean to say that eternal glory will far outweigh all our troubles?

⊖ apply

11. Look again at the reasons for Christian suffering:
- to display God's power (v 7)
- to bring glory to God and the gospel to others (v 15)
- to focus our minds on eternity (v 16-19)

How can we keep these things uppermost in our minds, so that we are ready to stand firm when suffering comes?

⊡ explore more

optional

❯ Read Philippians 4 v 4-13.

When Paul wrote his letter to the church at Philippi, he was chained day and night to guards in a Roman prison because of his faith in Jesus Christ (1 v 12-13).
- *How does Paul feel in the middle of his suffering?*

• *Why is he able to feel like this? Look at...*

v 6-7

v 8

v 10

• *How does this tie in with what we have learned from 2 Corinthians?*

• *What has Paul 'learned' (v 12), and what does this tell us about how we find contentment?*

• *What is 'the secret of being content in any and every situation', even in hardship (v 13)?*

⬆ pray

• Thank God for the life of the apostle Paul—for his example of contentment in many difficult situations, and for his teaching, which can lead us to contentment in suffering as well.

• Confess times when you have been unwilling to trust the promises of God. Read some of these truths again, and ask God to help you live by them. 2 Cor 1 v 3-4; 2 Cor 4 v 17; Phil 4 v 13.

• Pray for Christians, in your community or abroad, who are facing severe hardship. Pray that they will find contentment in the compassion, hope and strength of God.

Luke 6 v 12-26

THE SECRET OF TRUE HAPPINESS

⊕ talkabout

1. Most parents will say they want their children to be happy. What are they hoping for when they say this?

⊕ investigate

In Session Two we saw that only the gift of Jesus Christ can heal the hunger of our dissatisfied hearts—'He who comes to me will never go hungry, and he who believes in me will never be thirsty.' In this final session, Jesus teaches His followers the pattern of true discipleship.

> **Read Luke 6 v 12-26**

2. What do the words 'blessed' (v 20-22) and 'woe' (v 24-26) mean?

3. Jesus talks about His disciples being poor, hungry and weeping (v 20-21). What does He mean? Put your initial thoughts below, and then complete the table over the page.

Luke 6	What do other verses tell us?	What does Jesus mean in Luke 6?
Poor (v 20)	Matthew 5 v 3	
	Luke 7 v 21-22 • How did Jesus help the poor?	
Hungry (v 21)	Matthew 5 v 6	
	John 6 v 35 • How did Jesus feed the hungry?	
Weeping (v 21)	Luke 7 v 36-39 • What kind of weeping does Jesus commend?	

4. According to Jesus, how can His disciples be happy when they are poor, hungry and weeping?

• Can we expect this happiness now, or only in the future (see v 20b)?

5. Look at verses 22-23. What does Jesus expect to happen to His disciples, and why?

6. Jesus tells His disciples how they can respond to the hatred they will suffer because of Him (v 23a). Have you ever experienced this?

• What does this tell us about the kind of joy that Jesus promises His disciples?

7. In verse 23 Jesus tells His followers to look forward and look back. To what—and how does this help?

⮊ apply

8. Imagine that someone asks you: '*Can Jesus bring me true happiness?*' How will you answer them?

9. If you were a parent, what would you want most for your children? In what way do Jesus' words here change the answer to question 1?

⊡ **investigate**

10. **Look at verses 24-26.** When Christians see the apparently happy, carefree lives of non-Christians around them, what should they tell themselves?

⊡ **explore more**

❭ **Read Psalm 23**

- *What is promised in this psalm?*

- *What circumstances are mentioned?*

- *How does David's experience fit with the words of Jesus in Luke 6?*

- *What is the reason why David can be content and happy in all circumstances?*

- *What does it mean, that 'the Lord is my shepherd'?*

⊟ **apply**

11. According to Jesus, His disciples can experience right now the kind of happiness that makes them 'leap for joy' (v 23), despite the painful and difficult things that they must inevitably go through as His disciples. When and where is this kind of joy seen in your church?

- Why don't we see more of this kind of joy in our churches?

getting personal

Can people around you see that you are 'blessed', no matter what happens to you? Do they know that it is because of Jesus, your good shepherd? Has anyone ever asked you to explain the hope that you have (1 Peter 3 v 14-15)? How might God use you to bring others into the blessing that only Jesus can give?

pray

• Think about on what you have learned about **yourself** during these Bible studies. Ask God to help you find contentment in those areas of your life where you struggle the most.

• Reflect on what you have learned about **God** during these studies. Spend time in praise and thanksgiving for all the wonderful things that He has done and will do for you in Jesus Christ.

CONTENTMENT
healing the hunger
of our hearts

LEADER'S GUIDE

Leader's Guide

Introduction

Leading a Bible study can be a bit like herding cats—everyone has a different idea of what the passage could be about, and a different line of enquiry that they want to pursue. But a good group leader is more than someone who just referees this kind of discussion. You will want to:

★ **correctly understand** and handle the Bible passage. But also…

★ **encourage and train** the people in your group to do this for themselves. Don't fall into the trap of spoon-feeding people by simply passing on the information in the Leader's Guide. Then…

★ make sure that no Bible study is finished without everyone **knowing how the passage is relevant for them**. What changes do you all need to make in the light of the things you have been learning? And finally…

★ encourage the group to turn all that has been learned and discussed into **prayer**.

Your Bible-study group is unique, and you are likely to know better than anyone the capabilities, backgrounds and circumstances of the people you are leading. That's why we've designed these guides with a number of optional features. If they're a quiet bunch, you might want to spend longer on **talkabout**. If your time is limited you can choose to skip **explore more**, or get people to look at these questions at home. Can't get enough of Bible study? Well, some studies have optional extra homework projects. As leader, you can adapt and select the material to the needs of your particular group.

So what's in the Leader's Guide?

The main thing that this Leader's Guide will help you to do is to understand the major teaching points in the passage you are studying, and how to apply them. As well as guidance on the questions, the Leader's Guide for each session contains the following important sections:

THE BIG IDEA

One key sentence will give you the main point of the session. This is what you should be aiming to have fixed in people's minds as they leave the Bible study. And it's the point you need to head back towards when the discussion goes off at a tangent.

SUMMARY

An overview of the passage, including plenty of useful historical background information.

OPTIONAL EXTRA

Usually this is an introductory activity, that ties in with the main theme of the Bible study, and is designed to 'break the ice' at the beginning of a session. Or it may be a 'homework project' that people can tackle during the week.

So let's take a look at the various features of a Good Book Guide.

talkabout: each session kicks off with a discussion question, based on the group's opinions or experiences. It's designed to get people talking and thinking in a general way about the main subject of the Bible study.

⊥ **investigate**: the first thing that you and your group need to know is what the Bible passage is about, which is the purpose of these questions. But watch out —people may come up with answers based on their experiences or teaching they have heard in the past, without referring to the passage at all. It's amazing how often we can get through a Bible study without actually looking at the Bible!

And if you're stuck for an answer the Leader's Guide contains guidance on questions. These are the answers to which you need to direct your group. This information isn't meant to be read out to people—ideally, you want them to discover these answers from the Bible for themselves. Sometimes optional follow-up questions (see ⊗ in guidance on questions) are included, to help you help your group get to the answer.

⊞ **explore more**: these questions generally point people to other relevant parts of the Bible. They are useful for helping your group to see how the passage fits into the 'big picture' of the whole Bible. These sections are **OPTIONAL**—only use them if you have time. Remember, it's better to finish in good time having really grasped one big thing from the passage, than to try and cram everything in.

⊟ **apply**: we want to encourage you to spend more time working at application— too often, it is simply tacked on at the end. In the **Good Book Guides**, apply sections are mixed in with the investigate sections of the study. We hope that people will realise that application is not just an optional extra, but rather, the whole purpose of studying the Bible. We do Bible study so that our lives can be changed by what we hear from God's Word. If you skip the application, the Bible study hasn't achieved its purpose.

These questions draw out practical lessons that we can all learn from the Bible passage. You can review what has been learned so far, and think about practical differences that this should make in our churches and our lives. The group gets the opportunity to talk about what they personally have learned.

A ⊡ **getting personal** section can be done at home, or you could allocate a few moments of quiet reflection for each person to think about specific changes that they need to make and pray through in their own lives.

Why not have a time for reporting back at the beginning of the following session, so that everyone can be encouraged and challenged by one another to make application a priority?

⬆ **pray**: In Acts 4 v 25-30 the first Christians quoted Psalm 2 as they prayed in response to the persecution of the apostles by the Jewish religious leaders. Today however, it's not as common for Christians to base prayers on the truths of God's word as it once was. As a result, our prayers tend to be weak, superficial and self-centred rather than bold, visionary and God-centred.

The prayer section is based on what has been learned from the Bible passage. How different our prayer times would be if we were genuinely responding to what God has said to us through His word.

See note on page 71 regarding some extra materials available online.

1 Ecclesiastes
OUR HUNGRY HEARTS

THE BIG IDEA

Since the rebellion of humans against God, life 'under the sun' is meaningless because God has made it so. We cannot hope to find contentment in this world alone, because only God can give meaning to our lives.

SUMMARY

This series begins with our experience of discontent, by highlighting some of the main themes of the Old Testament book of Ecclesiastes. This investigation of the meaning of life was written by the 'Teacher' (1 v 1), someone who appears to have had immense wealth, status, achievements and wisdom, and who lived at a time of peace for Israel. (Some identify the teacher as King Solomon, but we're not told.) Surely someone like this could find contentment!

The Teacher sets out to explore 'all that is done under heaven', and ends up tormented by the meaninglessness of life. Everything that gives a human life meaning is out of reach. He knows that it is better to live a wise and good life, but because everyone comes to the same end (death), he can't explain why wisdom and righteousness are better. Clearly, it is better to be alive than dead (9 v 4). But if we cannot enjoy our lives—something beyond the control of any of us (9 v 11)— then it would be better never to have been born (6 v 3). The Teacher realises that enjoyment of life is a good gift of God (5 v 19), but it seems only possible when we are not reflecting on our lives (v 20), and ultimately, it can only be enjoyment of a meaningless life (9 v 9). He concludes that we must go beyond the sun—we must remember, fear and obey God, our Creator and Judge.

The phrases 'under heaven' and 'under the sun', used repeatedly throughout the book, tell us that the Teacher is investigating what happens in this world and this life. Mostly, he does not include heaven or eternity (ie: God's plan and view of things) in his investigation. This is how most people choose to live most of the time—as if there is no God—and it seems the Teacher wants to show the futility and hopelessness of living like this.

This session aims to show that we cannot find contentment in the things of this life and this world alone (even though God has given us many good things to enjoy), since creation has been blighted by the Fall (Adam and Eve's rebellion against God, and its consequences). The session looks at why death makes meaning impossible for us to achieve. We are challenged to see that our 'best hope'— enjoyment of the things that God has given us—is, in the end, pitiful. We need to bring God fully into the picture.

On a practical level, there is guidance on how to help both those who despair of life in this world, and those who are unthinkingly happy. On a personal level, we are challenged to seek contentment 'beyond the sun'. The questions of how we can do this, and how the problems of death and fallenness can be overcome are covered in Session Two.

GUIDANCE ON QUESTIONS

1. Ask your group to imagine such a situation, if that would be more appropriate. Answers may include: worrying or stressful thoughts; a painful memory that suddenly comes into our minds; an intrusion (eg: mobile phone) that brings us back to down to earth; the thought that your blissful enjoyment can't last; etc. Point out that it is often our thoughts, rather than events, that ruin our contentment.

2. The Teacher seems to be in despair about life. He repeatedly describes it as 'meaningless' (v 2, 14), and also as 'wearisome' (v 8).
• Some people may be surprised that someone so rich and wise can be so negative about life. Others may not be surprised, having come across similar examples of despair in the lives of rich, famous and successful people of our own times.

3. It might seem daunting to try to get your group to work through the whole of Ecclesiastes, but it lays the foundation for understanding why life is filled with discontent. Split the group up to work through the table, and report back your findings.

4. APPLY: Allow people to share their own ideas. Obvious answers include drugs, alcohol, spending sprees, hooliganism, workaholism, etc. But what about more socially acceptable ways of seeking meaning for our lives eg: through having children, making a good home, endless shopping? Discuss whether these are any more effective in overcoming the problems highlighted in question 3. For

What did he try out?	What did he discover?
1 v 16-18; 2 v 12-16 wisdom and folly	1 v 18: The wiser you are, the more sorrow you have.
	2 v 16: The wise man dies and is forgotten, just like the fool.
2 v 1-3: pleasure	v 11: Although he enjoyed these things (v 10), he failed to achieve anything meaningful, and that is what deprived him of satisfaction and contentment.
2 v 4-6: projects	
2 v 7-8: possessions	
2 v 9: prestige	
2 v 17-23: work	v 18-19: No matter how hard or how well you work, everything you achieve must be left to someone who has not worked for it and may well ruin it all.
	v 23: All you are guaranteed to get from work is pain, grief and stress.

example, our children and grandchildren may remember us, but for how long will that continue? It doesn't seem enough to give the kind of meaningful existence that the Teacher was searching for.

5. There is nothing wrong with enjoying the good things of life, but the Teacher wants us to understand that, whether we know it or not, this is the gift of God. See also 3 v 12-13; 5 v 18-20.

6. Death—everyone is going to die. We all share a common destiny, regardless of how we have lived (v 2). We don't even have control over when we will die (v 11-12). It is better to be alive than dead (v 4-6), and yet, nothing meaningful is achieved when we are alive. In the same way, it is better to be wise than to be a fool, and yet, 'under the sun' (see comments in summary on page 46 for the meaning of this phrase) nothing is gained by being wise because the wise man and the fool both die (2 v 13-16). Death is the greatest problem that we are up against in trying to achieve a meaningful life; it destroys everything:

7. The best that we can hope for is to enjoy what we can now. There are plenty of enjoyable things that God has given us, but don't expect or hope to find any meaning in life. 'Enjoy life ... all your meaningless days' (v 9).

8. In these important verses the Teacher tells us that God Himself has laid a heavy burden on humans—a sense of meaninglessness that persists whatever we do. God has given us a desire for beauty, immortality and understanding that cannot be satisfied in this world (3 v 10-11). He has deliberately designed things this way—He wants us to feel that life is meaningless, and experience the despair of that. (See also 3 v 18 and 6 v 1-2.)

9. APPLY: This is answered in Explore More (see Romans 1 v 18, 21-24), but if your group is opting out of this section, you will need to briefly explain God's response to the rebellion of the first humans (Genesis 1 – 3); He allowed His relationship with humans, their relationship with each other, and their relationship with creation to be ruined. Humans now experience nature as hostile and dangerous; our relationships with each other are painful and abusive; our relationship with God is non-existent—at best, we are searching for someone we don't know without knowing how to find Him. However, this is not just retaliation—there is a purpose in all this: we humans need to confront the truth and scale of our problems, before we can be helped. Compare the words of Jesus in Mark 2 v 17.

EXPLORE MORE: Romans 1 v 18-25
This passage makes explicit what is implicit in Ecclesiastes—that discontent is the result of living in our fallen world. But more than that, discontent is part of the judgment of frustration that God has placed on the fallen world. Even this is merciful, however, as it is designed to wake us up to the reality of God's coming judgment, and therefore to look to God for salvation. It may be unrealistic to do this study in the same session, so an alternative might be to encourage people to look at the passage during the week, and answer the questions for themselves at home.
• People know about God's eternal power and divine nature (everything that makes Him God, and immeasurably greater than humans).

- This can be clearly seen from creation—the astonishing design that is seen in nature requires a designer who must be infinitely greater than anything seen in nature.
- People should glorify God (the only appropriate way for human creatures to treat their Creator) and give thanks to Him.
- Instead, humans suppress the truth about God (v 18), they refuse to glorify or thank Him (v 21), and they treat created things like gods instead (v 23).
- They do this because they want to live godless and wicked lives ie: living as they want, not as God wants them to.
- The result is that God is angry with humans (v 18) and He shows His anger by allowing them to do what they want and to reap the consequences of their wickedness—futile thinking, darkened hearts (v 21), folly (v 22), slavery to their desires, degrading of their bodies (v 24) and belief in lies (v 25).

From this passage we can see that God has spoiled our experience of life in this world, and made our lives feel meaningless, because of His anger at our wickedness and rejection of Him.

10. The Teacher's conclusion is that we should bring God into the picture. We need to adopt the right attitude towards God—we should fear Him (12 v 13)—and we need to live accordingly ('keep his commandments' v 13).

- Ideally, we should bring God into the picture when we are young (12 v 1), because we will get more depressed, timid, and unresponsive as we grow older (see 12 v 2-5). But we should certainly bring God into the picture before we die (12 v 6-7). After death, it is too late to do anything.

11. APPLY: Get people to summarise what they have learned this session, and choose from the optional extra questions below as appropriate for your group.

Summary: We cannot find contentment in our world because everything has been spoiled as the consequence of human rebellion against God. Most importantly, we all face death.

It is right to enjoy the many good gifts from God, but we can only enjoy them if we don't think too much about the meaning of life. So however we live, we cannot find contentment 'under the sun'—we have to look 'beyond the sun' to God Himself for answers.

☑ **How can the Teacher's wisdom help us to deal with our own discontent?** We tend to focus on the thing that appears to be causing the problem—relationships, work, church etc. But improving that situation, whatever it may be, will not automatically result in contentment. We need to face up to the truth that we live in a fallen world, and our enjoyment of the many good things that we have in this life will always be blighted, because God does not want us to be satisfied with this world. Our discontent should be like a 'goad' (12 v 11) that turns us towards our Creator. Without that first step, we can't be helped.

☑ **How can the Teacher's wisdom guide our relationships with those who suffer from discontent and despair, as well as those who are enjoying life without God?** He helps us to understand why people can feel utter despair about life, even when they have plenty of good things (eg: 6 v 1-6). Be aware that some may be clinically depressed and need medical help. Others may 'talk themselves' into a state of negativity, by failing to count their blessings, focusing on their own selfish desires, cutting themselves off from those who can help them etc, and can be helped by changing their thought-patterns and lifestyles. However, it is still true that life in our physical universe is meaningless, regardless of who we are or how we live. Therefore it is right and proper for us to feel blighted, even in our enjoyment—it makes us face up to the truth about our lives. Those who are enjoying life also need to hear this. We know that days of darkness will come to all of us, and good friends will want to warn others out of their complacency.

OPTIONAL EXTRA

One person describes a blissful situation or experience. Everyone else suggests things that are likely to ruin it.

- *Sunning yourself by a private pool on a paradise island*

tropical bugs; danger of heatstroke; realising how much flab is on display; remembering that this time next week you will be back in the office; realising that most people on your island live below the poverty line.

THE ONLY FOOD THAT SATISFIES

THE BIG IDEA

Jesus, the bread of life, promises that all who believe in Him will never go hungry or be thirsty, and that He will raise us up on the last day; with Jesus we can begin to know contentment in this world.

SUMMARY

In the last session we learned that discontent with life 'under the sun' can be good, because it shows that we need to start living for God. This session investigates some words of Jesus about how we should do that, spoken soon after He miraculously fed 5,000 people on the shores of Lake Galilee. This was a sign, pointing to the fact that Jesus is the bread of life, sent down from heaven. The heart of Jesus' message is very simple: 'He who comes to me will never go hungry, and he who believes in me will never be thirsty … and I will raise him up at the last day' (v 35, 40).

Despite the miracles, people seriously misunderstood Jesus' identity and mission. Excited by the prospect of someone who could provide for their earthly needs (v 14-15), they failed to see what the miraculous signs were pointing to (v 26)—that Jesus is the one sent from heaven, with God's seal of approval (v 27). He came to do something far greater than providing physical bread—to bring eternal life to the whole world. But on hearing this, some people gave up on Jesus and His teaching (v 60, 66). Their small ambitions (v 26), stubborn insistence on their own agenda (v 15), and prejudice against Jesus (v 42)

led them to reject the promise of eternal life. But Jesus has not failed in His mission. No one can come to Him unless the Father has enabled them to (v 44, 65). Those who do believe in Him have in fact been chosen by Him (v 69-70).

However, God's initiative in opening people's eyes to understand who Jesus truly is does not absolve us of any responsibility to act. Jesus tells people to 'work for food that endures to eternal life', rather than work for 'food that spoils' (v 27). This means believing in Him (v 29, 35, 40).

This session challenges us to turn to Jesus as the first response to our discontent, to trust that He can and will satisfy our hunger and thirst, but also to face up to the reality that we must wait for the last day, before we can enjoy a life that is all we have ever dreamed of and more. All this means that we need to give up working for 'food that spoils'. We discover what it means to feed on Jesus—the bread of life—and why Jesus used this image. There is also an opportunity to reflect on why people ultimately reject the wonderful gift of Jesus, and what we need to accept Him ourselves.

Note: This passage confronts people with the doctrine of election (God chooses those who are saved) from the lips of Jesus. Some people find it difficult to believe that God chooses to save some people and not others because this seems unfair. It may be helpful to spend some time on this issue after the session or arrange another time for this. For a brief but biblical response, see the chapter entitled 'Election' in *Bitesize Theology* by Peter Jeffery, published by Evangelical Press. Or refer to a good systematic theology eg: Chapter 32 of Systematic Theology by Wayne Grudem, published by IVP. (Available from www.thegoodbook.co.uk)

GUIDANCE ON QUESTIONS

1. 'Reflex' praying reveals what people subconsciously believe about God. People generally think that He should fix their problems, reward their 'goodness' and remove any suffering. Their wishes are likely to be very much focused on material and emotional wellbeing in this life.

⊜ **When do you instinctively turn to prayer, and what do you pray for?**

2. They want to be fed and eat their fill (v 26). They want Jesus to reproduce God's miracle of providing food for Israel in the desert (v 30-31).

3. Jesus wants something even better for them—He wants them to have eternal life (v 27).
• He thinks their ambitions are too small.

4. We have to believe in the one God has sent ie: Jesus (v 29). People often understand 'the work of God' (v 29) to mean some special religious duty, mission or self-sacrificial act which will please God, but Jesus is clear that the work of God is faith in Jesus. Believing in Jesus doesn't just mean accepting as true the things that Jesus said or that the Bible claims about Him. It also involves changing your life to live in agreement with those beliefs. Eg: you may accept that Jesus is the Son of God, but if you don't show any interest in what He has said, you fail to treat Him as the Son of God. This shows that you don't truly

believe in Him. Jesus is not saying that these people should give up earning a livelihood, but that the focus of their energy and life's work should be to find and receive eternal life.
• We can only get eternal life from Jesus. He is unique. And because none of us have access to eternal life ourselves, it shows us that He is not an ordinary human. Only God is eternal, so Jesus must be from God.

5. v 14-15: The people recognise that Jesus is the fulfilment of God's promise to Israel, (to raise up another prophet like Moses—see Deuteronomy 18 v 18), but in their view, this was a promise of a political leader who would again liberate Israel from (Roman) oppression. If they had truly understood who Jesus was, how would they have dared to even think about forcing Him to be their king?
v 30-31: They want Him to keep doing spectacular miracles. Despite all that they have seen, when they come to Him and only hear Him teaching instead of seeing more miracles, they doubt that He is the one sent from God, and the Prophet who is greater than Moses.
v 41-42: Rather than accept the evidence of the miraculous signs, the Jews prefer to be guided by their own prejudices about someone sent from heaven. They conclude that Jesus cannot be sent from heaven because He is one of them.
• If they had correctly thought about what the miraculous signs were pointing to, they would have realised that Jesus *must* be one who had come with the approval of God the Father, and therefore, that He would be able to give them 'food that endures to eternal life' (v 27) They should have seen, not that He could keep them well-fed until death, but that He could help them overcome death itself.

6. APPLY: People may share their own experiences of misunderstandings about Jesus. Otherwise, here are a couple of ideas to get the ball rolling.

The **'prosperity gospel'** teaches that faith in Jesus will bring you financial or academic success, prosperity, healing etc. None of these things are promised to Christians in the New Testament. On the contrary, in this life Christians are promised hardships and persecution!

Many preach Jesus as an inspiration or model for curing social problems, such as poverty, injustice, and inequality. While these may be important issues, they miss the point about who Jesus is.

Even genuine Christians can make the mistake of majoring on how Christianity improves your relationships or lifestyle, when they share the Christian message with others.

Note: Beware the temptation to look down on the people of Jesus' time, as if we would never have misunderstood Jesus in the way they did—we are just as prone to want instant gratification here and now as the crowd in John 6.

When we truly understand who Jesus is, then we will seek from Him the things that only He can give—forgiveness of sins, peace with God, treasures in heaven, eternal life—rather than worldly success, prosperity and satisfaction. This will be evident in the way that we pray—our prayers will be a reflection of the new relationship with God that Jesus Christ has made possible for us, (expressing our gratitude, confession, love, delight, adoration, thoughts and longings) rather than just a shopping list of our needs and wants (compare answers to question 1).

7. The following questions may help your group to answer this question.

• What is the difference between Jesus giving us the bread of life and Jesus being the bread of life? If Jesus Himself is the bread of life, we cannot have eternal life without becoming involved personally with the God/man Jesus. This is completely different from other religions, where people are given rules or rituals by prophets who claim to be sent from God. The heart of true Christianity is not following directions given by Jesus Christ, but a relationship with the risen Jesus Himself.

• What does the image of bread tell us about our need of Jesus? Jesus is as vital to our hopes of eternal life as bread (food) is for physical life. Without Jesus, we simply cannot have eternal life.

• What does the image of feeding on Jesus, the bread of life, tell us about a Christian's relationship with Jesus Christ? Jesus is not just a way into eternal life, so that after we've 'got' eternal life, we can forget all about Him. His relationship with us is a source of constant spiritual nourishment, so we should come to Him continually (just as we eat daily). In fact, just as food is absorbed into the body, Jesus becomes part of us (ie: He chooses to be identified with believers), as we also become a part of Him (v 56).

8. Jesus is not talking about physical hunger or thirst—He is referring to the persistent dissatisfaction and emptiness that come from living in a fallen world. The problems of alienation from God, meaninglessness and death are solved once for all by Jesus' own death on the cross. When we trust in Him, our spiritual needs can be met. Never again will we have to know that we are cut off from God, that our lives are meaningless, and that death will destroy us.

Note: At this point it may be helpful to discuss what 'eternal life' means. Look at v 54—to those who are united with Him, Jesus promises both eternal life now and resurrection at the last day ie: eternal life is more than living forever beyond the grave.

• **What exactly is the 'eternal life' that a Christian has now?** Eternal life = being saved from our sins and enjoying a relationship of love and grace with our heavenly Father (see Ephesians 2 v 1-7).

• Our first response to discontent must be to turn to Jesus, to trust the promise that He gives in v 35, and to seek contentment in what He alone can give us—salvation from sin, forgiveness from God, reconciliation with our heavenly Father, the hope of resurrection etc.—all the things that are summed up in the words 'eternal life'.

EXPLORE MORE: John 4 v 4-19; 25-29
This can be offered as optional homework.
• Jesus offers the woman 'living water'— whoever drinks it will never thirst again.
• Jesus gives this living water, so to get it we must come and ask Him.
• The woman is thinking only about her own physical need for water, and she doubts that Jesus could be greater than her forefather, Jacob.
• She begins to believe that Jesus is the Christ (the one that the Old Testament promised would be sent to Israel from God), and she acts on her growing belief by going back to her town and telling others about Jesus.
• Jesus' promise is for everyone, regardless of how they have lived (the woman had had five husbands and was

now co-habiting with another man), what nationality they are (she was a despised Samaritan), and how they are viewed by people around them (in accordance with the custom of the time, the disciples looked down on her because she was a woman).
• Jesus' living water will become a spring of water in us, welling up to eternal life. Our character and our daily life will be changed to reflect what Jesus has done for us, and to bring eternal life to others.

9. The people were taken up with what Jesus could do for them, rather than who He was. They wanted someone who would give them as much food as they needed now (v 26), and who would also satisfy their political ambitions (v 14-15), neither of which Jesus was willing to promise. By seeking to satisfy these desires they were blind to their true need, and to the wonder of Jesus' promise.

It seems that they were offended, not so much by the promise of eternal life, but by Jesus' claim to be the one sent by the Father from heaven. In their thinking, how could an ordinary Galilean man, whose family they knew, be the only one who has seen the Father, and the only one who gives eternal life?

Jesus used vivid picture language to convey that we are utterly dependent on Jesus for eternal life, as much as we depend on food and water for physical survival (v 57). More than this, we do not even have the power to come to Jesus of our own accord—we need God to enable us (v 65). The Jews preferred to rely on their own achievement in keeping God's law, by which they could feel superior to others, rather than helpless and dependent.

10. They understood that there was no one else who could help them (v 68). Only Jesus was able to give them eternal life because only He was the Holy One of God (v 69).

• This kind of faith can only come from God (v 65). Simon Peter could say this only because Jesus had chosen him (v 70). If we want to believe as Simon Peter did, we must ask God to open our eyes.

11. APPLY: Our first response to discontent must be to come to Jesus. He has promised that those who come to Him and believe in Him will never go hungry or be thirsty (v 35). Ask yourself: 'Am I discontent because I am working for food that spoils—looking for contentment in this fallen world that will always disappoint us? Do I trust that Jesus

can and will give me eternal life? Do I understand what that means? If not, what do I need to do about it?'

• People should summarise the big picture that they have learned so far from Sessions One and Two.

OPTIONAL EXTRA
Have a 'bread banquet'. Set out as many different kinds of bread as you can (or invite each person to bring along their favourite kind of bread). Include bloomers, bagels, tortillas, naans, pittas sourdough, fruitbread etc. See if people can identify bread from different parts of the world. Take a vote on the best bread. As you try out different breads, discuss how often you eat it and the different ways in which you use it.

1 Timothy 6 v 3-19
CONTENT WITH WHAT WE HAVE

THE BIG IDEA
The love of money is the root of all kinds of evil, and a trap of the devil, but godliness with contentment is great gain.

SUMMARY
The next few sessions investigate the experience of Christians living in a fallen world where everyone is subject to pain, difficulty and frustration. Christians are those who believe in Jesus—the one who said: 'He who comes to me will never go

hungry, and he who believes in me will never be thirsty'. So how can it be possible for a Christian to be satisfied and content, while still living in a fallen world? First, we deal with the subject of wealth and possessions by looking at Paul's first letter to Timothy.

The study begins by looking at Paul's concerns about false teachers in the church. Although this may not seem immediately relevant, it soon becomes clear that these people are motivated by greed for wealth, highlighting the spiritually lethal consequences of discontent with what we have. Dissatisfaction with our standard of living, according to this passage, can finally end in heresy, evil behaviour and loss of faith.

By contrast, Paul commends 'godliness with contentment' as a great treasure. The godly and contented person is someone who understands things as they really are—we bring nothing into the world and can take nothing out so we have no rights to anything that we own; rather, we have received an abundance of gifts from God, enough for our needs and usually far more. The godly and contented person is liberated from slavery to getting things they don't need, saved from the tragedy of working for things that they cannot take out of this world, and has their eyes opened to see God's goodness. They will escape the trap of the devil that destroys those who love money.

Paul outlines the steps by which Christians escape this trap of the devil. We need to flee from the old way of life—chasing after wealth; we need to fill our lives with pursuing righteousness, faith, love, endurance and gentleness; we need to fight our way through the Christian life; and we need to take hold of the gift of eternal life that Christ has won for us. Paul reminds Christians
• that they live their lives in the sight of both their Creator and Saviour.
• of the example of the Lord Jesus Christ.
• that the battle is not forever, because Christ's return is certain.
• of who God really is—'the blessed and only Ruler, the King of kings and Lord of lords'.

It is these things that will keep us going.

In this session people are challenged to think about how the love of money may be disguised in their own lives, and to take seriously the warnings that Paul gives to the rich—which includes all of us who live in the west. There is also an opportunity to think about practical ways in which we can become rich in good deeds, by showing generosity and willingness to share.

GUIDANCE ON QUESTIONS

1. Likely answers include:
fashion and peer pressure—so we can be just like everyone else.
asserting our identity—so we can stand out from the crowd and be noticed.
the attention and compliments that new possessions can attract.
status and prestige—everyone can see how rich / successful / tasteful we are, etc.

Not every reason is self-centred—we may enjoy something because of its sentimental value/memories; because it opens up new opportunities; because it enables us to help or share enjoyment with others; or because we can see that it is a good gift from our heavenly Father. The second part of the question will show how much the enjoyment of our possessions is due to what others think of us.

2. This question highlights the grave consequences of the love of money, beginning with the consequences and working back to the cause.
• **Fruit:** these people teach false doctrines and do not agree with sound instruction or godly teaching (v 3); they display envy, strife, malicious talk, evil suspicions and constant friction (v 4, 5). Though these faults are, sadly, found in some churches, they are very far from what any Christian should be.

- **Character:** they are conceited, ignorant and have an unhealthy interest in pointless controversies and quarrels (v 4); they have corrupt minds (v 5).
- **What drives them:** the desire for financial gain (v 5). It may seem surprising that people like this want to be church leaders, but as Paul points out, these people see church as a way of getting rich.

3. People may initially think of something like love or outstanding faith.
- Paul, however, identifies 'godliness with contentment' as the key characteristic that will distinguish a man of God from a false teacher, because this is what will prevent him from travelling down the route of the false teachers.

4. The desire to get rich is far from harmless—it is 'a trap', in which people follow harmful and foolish desires that bring them to ruin and destruction (v 9). Those who are content, however, will be immune from such desires, and will avoid the trap. In Paul's other references to a 'trap' (1 Timothy 3 v 7 and 2 Timothy 2 v 26), he speaks about the devil's trap, in which the devil takes people captive to do his will. The devil's will is to ruin and destroy everything that God has made, loves, and plans to bless. So it is the devil who lies behind our discontent and desire to get rich.

Like a trap hidden from its victim, the love of money may not seem especially dangerous for the Christian, in comparison with other sins. However, **if we give in** to the love of money, we will find that **we can't give it up**. It will corrupt our thinking, our actions, and ultimately, our faith. We will be plunged into ruin and destruction (v 9). This is clearly more than merely financial ruin, since Paul goes on to

point out that the love of money has caused some people to wander from the faith (v 10)—this is the ultimate ruin and destruction that the devil is seeking. It is vital to underline how lethal discontent and the love of money may be to our eternal destiny. We should never minimise the gravity of discontent, or use the excuses of personality, upbringing or culture to avoid dealing with it.

Note: Can a Christian wander away from the faith? Isn't it true that 'once saved = always saved'. Romans 8 v 37-39 is often used to back up this view. It is right to say that a true Christian can never be lost, but a true Christian is someone who perseveres in the faith. So, earlier in Romans 8, Paul encourages Christians to live according to the Spirit, which involves the painful process of putting to death 'the misdeeds of the body', because 'if you live according to the sinful nature, you will die' (v 13). If there were no danger that people who believe themselves to be Christians could ultimately be lost, Paul would not have to say these things.

5. APPLY: Allow the group to share their own ideas of how people disguise the love of money. You could allow a few moments for quiet reflection, in which people can examine their own hearts (see getting personal). Here are some suggested answers:
- Many people tell themselves that their attitude to money is one of 'being sensible'—looking after their family, or putting themselves in a position where they can help others.
- People may justify an affluent lifestyle on the grounds that they are trying to reach people with a similar standard of living for Christ;
- Some Christians—unaware of the dangers that Paul highlights here—may

naively assume that it is better to have money in the hands of a Christian than a non-Christian;

- Many Christians misunderstand the OT promises to Israel, which rewarded faith and obedience with physical blessings such as prosperity and health. They assume that God will do exactly the same for Christians today (a teaching known as the 'prosperity gospel'). For them, enjoying and expecting wealth is part of showing faith in God. They don't realise that the Old Testament promises look forward to Christ—the promised physical blessings were only shadows of the true blessings that Christ would bring to His people. Christians can enjoy spiritual blessings in Christ that were not available to Israel. We will also enjoy physical blessings greater than those offered to Israel, but not until Jesus Christ returns.

6. Our rights: we brought nothing into the world (v 7), so we have no rights of ownership. Everything that we have is a gift of God, and most of us have a staggering abundance of gifts. When we understand this, we will not only be content, but also full of joy and gratitude to God, leading to godliness.

- **Our future:** we can take nothing out of the world (v 7), so a life devoted to acquiring possessions is utterly wasted. Contentment can save us from the horror of a whole life lived in the wrong direction.
- **Our needs:** when we are content, we can distinguish needs and wants (v 8). We can be content with little because we actually don't need very much. We can escape the slavery of sweating and struggling for a whole mass of things we don't need.

Note: People often view contentment as

stoical and 'stiff-upper-lip'—it's good for you but not much fun! Paul, by contrast, sees that the godly and contented person has something wonderful—it's 'great gain'. Help your group to get excited about 'godliness with contentment'—it brings true understanding and freedom from slavery to possessions.

7. v 11: *'Flee from all this'* ie: the evil and harm that results from pursuing riches (v 3-10). Notice that Paul first calls Timothy to turn away from wrong things. Being a Christian is not just about living a new way—it also involves giving up the old way. See the words of Jesus in Matthew 6 v 24-25.

v 11. *'Pursue righteousness, godliness, faith, love, endurance and gentleness.'* Giving up the love of money alone is not enough—Paul wants Timothy to fill his life with better and more important things that can be his because of Christ.

v 12. *'Fight the good fight of the faith.'* Paul chooses to describe the Christian life as a battle, because it will be hard and painful.

v 12. *'Take hold of the eternal life to which you were called.'* Here, Paul's words suggest that eternal life is not something that simply floats into our grasp as we sit and wait. Christ has won eternal life for us, but we must 'take hold of it'.

Note that the words 'flee', 'pursue', 'fight' and 'take hold' are all very active words. We don't escape the trap of the devil and we won't arrive at eternal life simply by drifting through life and waiting for the last day. We need to invest time and energy in turning from the wrong things and seeking the right ones. We need to be prepared for difficulties—weariness, discouragement, opposition, setbacks, etc.

Note: Christians who understand the importance of grace in our salvation may be disturbed by Paul's emphasis on human action here. However, it is no more a problem for Paul to teach human responsibility alongside God's grace than it was for Jesus Himself (see Session 2: Leader's Guide: Summary). God enables Christians to overcome the schemes of the devil, but only 'in Christ', which means they must keep going 'in Christ'.

8. v 13: *'In the sight of God … and of Christ Jesus'*: Christians will be encouraged to keep going if they know that both their Creator and their Saviour see everything that they do.
v 13: *'Christ Jesus … made the good confession'*: Jesus our Lord kept going in the most extreme of all trials, and Christians have the privilege of following Him by persevering in lesser trials.
v 14: *'until the appearing of our Lord Jesus Christ'*: Christians can keep going because the battle is not forever—one day Jesus Christ will return.
v 15-16: *God, the blessed and only Ruler…* Christians are privileged to have some understanding of who God is and how great He is (v 15-16)—who or what else can be worth living for?

9. Wealth can give people a wrong view of themselves—it makes them arrogant. They also put their trust in wealth rather than God, showing that, in their view, God is not to be trusted. They fail to see that God 'richly provides us with everything for our enjoyment'. Contrast how those who have 'godliness with contentment' view themselves and God (see question 6 above).

> ☑ Share examples that you have come across of ways in which rich people have shown arrogance, or trust in their wealth rather than God.

10. Paul wants people who are financially rich to view wealth in a different way altogether. They should be 'rich in good deeds' and so lay up lasting treasure that will continue into eternity, as opposed to money and possessions, which we cannot take out of this world. Notice the paradox: it is generosity and sharing that makes us truly rich.

11. APPLY: Encourage your group to come up with examples for discussion. Here are a couple of suggestions to get the ball rolling.
Examples of arrogance: churches in the west don't seem to recognise that we need Christians in other parts of the world—we can help them with our finance, literature, organisations and influence, but what can they do for us? So, how often do non-western speakers top the 'billing' of Christian conferences, and if they did, would as many people attend? Or how many western churches have two-way partnerships with non-western churches, who are not just receiving charity, but vital partners for our own spiritual wellbeing?
Examples of trust in wealth: churches react to problems by throwing people or money at them, rather than by praying together. Or by putting all their efforts into spectacular and exciting events, rather than good-quality, faithful Bible teaching.

• Paul's antidote is to be rich in good deeds—in particular, to be generous and willing to share. Get people to discuss what they, as part of a local church, could realistically and practically do, to show more generosity and willingness to share, not only in the local community but also internationally. Think about attitudes which may need to be challenged eg: saving for a rainy day.

12. This question is an opportunity for people to review and reflect on the session. Most in our society view wealth as desirable and the answer to all their problems, but Paul has shown that wealth brings deadly problems for the Christian, which we must be on our guard against.

EXPLORE MORE: James 4 v 1-10
This can be offered as optional homework.
• The problem is caused by our desires for things that we want—it's nothing to do with personal circumstances.
• Their relationship with God has broken down—either they don't ask God for anything, or they make selfish demands like spoilt children. But they are not interested in spending time with Him.
• They end up hating God.
• Like Paul, James tells Christians to turn from wrong (resist the devil—v 7) and to replace their wrong way of living with a new way (submit to God —v 7, come near to Him—v 8, purify themselves—v 8, humble themselves before Him—v 10). Like Paul, James uses active words—resist, come, wash, change.

• Additional insights: the devil will flee from us if we resist him (v 7); we need to wash and purify ourselves (v 8); God gives grace to the humble (v 6) and He lifts them up (v 10).

OPTIONAL EXTRA

1. *(Suitable for a group that know each other well).* Give people a piece of paper and ask them to write down their answer to the question: If you won a lottery jackpot of £20 million, what would you do? (If possible, choose an amount that someone has recently won that has been in the news). Give a time limit of one minute. Collect the answers; then read them out and see if people can guess who wrote the answer. It will be interesting to see how fully-formed people's answers are, indicating how much thinking they have already done on this question.

2. Get a selection of adverts, photos and articles from magazines and newspaper colour supplements that tempt us to feel discontent and to covet people's possessions. Or watch a selection of TV adverts. Discuss how some of these adverts disguise the pursuit of money and possessions to look like something more virtuous eg: doing the best for your children.

1 Corinthians 7 v 1-24
CONTENT WITH WHERE WE ARE

THE BIG IDEA

Don't put all your energy into changing the situation which you were in when you became a Christian; rather than aiming to better yourself, devote yourself to the gospel.

SUMMARY

Singleness, a disappointing marriage, or an unfulfilling job often lead to discontent. This session looks at how Christians should deal with 'un-ideal' situations. In the first-century church in Corinth, some people became Christians when they were already married to non-Christians, or were slaves, and Paul wrote to help them in these tricky situations.

In 1 Corinthians 7 Paul not only helps Christians facing un-ideal situations, but he also tackles false ideas of spirituality that were leading Christians into a number of errors. These false ideas could exacerbate difficult personal situations—people became dissatisfied with their situation when, in God's eyes, there was nothing wrong.

For instance, some had got hung up on the issue of whether or not it was more spiritual to be married or unmarried, or if married, whether it was more spiritual to abstain from sex (v 1-9). Others looked down on fellow-Christians who were married to non-Christians, and on the children of these mixed marriages (v 12-16). This climate of competitive spirituality among the various groups in the

Corinthian church made people constantly question their own situations, and focus their energies on change and improvement. This is the context in which Paul gives his key principle: 'Each one should remain in the situation which he was in when God called him' (v 20).

The session investigates four concerns or priorities of Paul:

- devotion to the Lord's affairs
- protection from Satan's temptations
- obedience to the Lord's commands
- bringing unbelievers to Christ

These can help us decide (if we are free to) whether to remain in a situation or seek change. These four priorities also help us to reassess the truth about our 'un-ideal' situations, and can transform our experience, by helping us to see things as God sees them ('real reality').

The session challenges us to think about whether we share Paul's priorities, and to help each other view things as God sees them. There is an opportunity to practise giving advice to fellow-Christians in the two case-studies at the end of the session.

GUIDANCE ON QUESTIONS

1. Paul's key principle that 'Each one should remain in the situation which he was in when God called him' (v 20—see question 4) is counter-cultural, and this question prepares people for that. At a frivolous level you can talk about cars or redecorating, before moving on to more important areas such as marriage, work, where you live, lifestyle, and even church. People change these things because they are seeking a better position in life—they want to be richer, more popular, happier, more comfortable etc. They follow the principle that the grass is always greener on the other side of the fence. Often people find it easier to run away—from mistakes, failure, wrong-doing, or bad relationships—and start again, failing to realise that they take the real problem (themselves) with them.

2. a=4; b=3; c=2; d=5; e=1

Note: v 3-7: Probably some in the Corinthian church thought it was more spiritual for Christians not to have sex. As a result, those who were unmarried might be contemplating unconsummated marriages, and those already married might feel under pressure to give up having sex. **v 10-11:** This question probably arose because some were saying that it was more spiritual to be unmarried, like Jesus. **v 12-14:** Single Christians were not to marry non-Christians—see v 39—so it is likely that when already married, one partner had become a Christian, but not the other.

3. a. It is good not to marry. *Reason* (v 32-35): An unmarried person can live in undivided devotion to the Lord.
v 9: It is better to marry than to burn with passion. *Motive*: Protection from sin.
b. v 5b: Do not deprive each other sexually (except under very limited conditions), so that Satan will not tempt you. *Motive*: Protection from sin.
c. v 10-11 (v 19b): The Lord commanded that married couples must not separate/divorce. *Motive*: Keeping God's commands.
d. and e. v 15b-16: Live in peace with your partner (either by staying in the marriage or by letting the marriage end,

depending on what the unbelieving partner wants), in the hope that through you they will be saved. *Motive*: Bringing non-Christians to Christ.

4. 'Each one should retain the place in life that the Lord assigned to him' (v 17). This principle is stated twice more in verses 20 and 24.

5. v 17: God has called each of us to our present situation, so He has a purpose for us there (see follow-up question below).

> ✉ **What can a Christian know about God's purposes (see Romans 8 v 28-30)?** In all things God works for the good of those who love Him, and that 'good' is that we should be made like His Son, Jesus (v 29).

• **v 19:** What is important is not what we, or others, think is important, but the things that God views as important—keeping His commands, rather than trying to improve our personal situation.
• **v 21-23:** Our situation is transformed by the fact that we are now Christians—we can view it in a completely different way.
• **v 24:** Each of us is responsible only to God in decisions about our present situation—we don't have to fit in with what other people expect.

6. APPLY: We don't have overt slavery in our society, but there are plenty of people that are overlooked, despised and shunned. For example: the elderly, the disabled and learning disabled, the uneducated, asylum seekers, travellers, etc. Allow the group to make suggestions relevant to their local community.

7. APPLY: Knowing what the Bible actually says is a good start. Having the courage, humility and wisdom to say it appropriately is the harder part. This may be a good time to make practical suggestions about things like prayer triplets or one-to-one mentoring.

EXPLORE MORE: 2 Kings 5 v 1-3, 9-15
• The young girl was a captive in a pagan land. She was a believer in the one true God, but surrounded by those who did not know Him, with no freedom to live as she chose.
• Likely answers include: resentful, depressed, determined to escape, willing to compromise, etc.
• She showed her faith in God by believing that He could and would heal her master, Naaman, if he visited the Lord's prophet in Israel. She spoke out about this even though she was just a foreign slave who could expect no hearing from her owners.
• God used the terrible circumstances of this young girl's exile and captivity to save Naaman and bring honour to His name in a foreign land. If she had given in to discontent eg: by running away or staying silent out of resentment to her master, God would not have been glorified through her faith.

8. In v 21 Paul tells slaves that if they can gain their freedom, they should do so. It's better to be free eg: because you can choose how to spend your time and use that freedom to meet with other Christians. However, Paul is not telling slaves to actively seek freedom; he simply encourages them to take any opportunities for freedom that come their way.

Paul is concerned that Christians will spend all their time and energy seeking to change their 'un-ideal' situation in life when, in fact, God has a purpose for them even in that situation, their reasons for wanting change are unimportant, and their desire for change comes from what

others think, rather than what God thinks of them. Paul does not want to see Christians spending all their time trying to outdo each other, according to wrong ideas of what is spiritual, while the Lord's work remains neglected.

9. APPLY: Max—his current job gives him plenty of time for involvement in youth work. The new job would mean leaving his church and ministry; he would almost certainly have to work far more hours and his uncle might not be sympathetic to commitments (like church) outside of work. The new job could also put him in the way of temptation eg: an affluent lifestyle; materialistic, pleasure-seeking colleagues. It will take time to find a new church and longer to establish the kind of relationships where he can be accountable to others. However, Max could take this new job with the aim of reaching city workers and even his uncle with the gospel. Think about whether this is the best way to go about this, and whether Max would be the right person for this kind of mission.

Kellie—it's great that she dreams of her own completely Christian family, but Kellie should leave this in God's hands. She needs to focus on obeying the Lord's commands. Christians may disagree about what is commanded in this situation. Some will argue that Kellie should not marry Joe because he is not a Christian (they may refer to a verse like 1 Corinthians 7 v 39). Others will argue that Kellie is, in effect, already married to the father of her child (they may refer to a verse like 1 Corinthians 6 v 16), so she should formalise her relationship by getting married. Since God's word does not address Kellie's situation directly, the important point is that *Kellie should* *decide,* not on the basis of her dreams for the future, but on the basis of what she understands is the right thing to do now. If Kellie believes that she is already 'married' to Joe, it is clear from 1 Corinthians 7 v 15-16 that she should stay with him, and pray that she or others can bring him to Christ.

10. APPLY: Max may be encouraged to stay in his dead-end job by realising that God's greatest purpose for His life is to bring others to faith and to build up Christian brothers and sisters in whatever way he is gifted. Max is pleasing God by being involved in his local church and by providing for his family—he doesn't need to worry about what his uncle thinks of his career choice.

Kellie needs to trust that God has a plan in allowing her to become a Christian in this particular situation—perhaps this is how Joe will come to Christ as well. She can be encouraged by knowing that she is in no way an inferior Christian. She should be helped to trust that God is able to bless her and to save her child in this situation as easily as in any other.

OPTIONAL EXTRA

Present the story of a Christian who has struggled in an un-ideal situation eg: ill-health, disability, injury, marriage problems, difficult family background, poverty, war etc. This may be someone in your church or a testimony from a book/the internet like the writer Joni Eareckson (paraplegic) or the hymn-writer William Cowper (severe depression). Make sure that the presentation highlights how God has been able to use this Christian, despite (or even because of) their un-ideal situation.

---

5 2 Corinthians 1 and 4
CONTENT WHEN LIFE IS HARD

THE BIG IDEA
The sufferings of Christ flow over into the lives of His followers, but if we trust in God, as Paul did, we can be content in all circumstances.

SUMMARY
Christians will face hardship—not only the difficulties and disappointments of living in a fallen world, but the suffering that comes specifically from following Jesus Christ—ridicule, hostility, ostracism, opposition, discrimination, slander, physical attacks, economic oppression, imprisonment, and ultimately perhaps, martyrdom. In the west Christians suffer far less persecution at present than their sisters and brothers in other parts of the world. Some western Christians have never heard the teaching that all followers of Christ will suffer as He did, and yet this is clear from both the words of Jesus and the experiences of His 'model' follower, the apostle Paul. This session shows that to follow Christ is to share to some extent in His sufferings.

The session looks at two passages from 2 Corinthians. In chapter 1 Paul refers to the hardships that he has suffered in his work for the gospel. He opens his letter in praise to God in the middle of troubles, and highlights the great things that God does for His people through the sufferings of His people. Paul returns to this theme in chapter 4, where he describes the gospel, taught by those like himself, as treasure in jars of clay—God shows Jesus Christ to the world in the weak and struggling lives of His servants. Here Paul sets out the reason why God sends hardship into the lives of Christians, the purpose which is achieved through our perseverance, and the hope of eternal glory that will makes all our suffering worthwhile.

People will be challenged in this session to put their trust in God's character and promises, to share God's understanding of what is achieved through the suffering of His people, and to look forward to eternal glory, confident that its arrival will more than compensate all of us for all our sufferings, so that for now, we can be content whatever comes our way.

GUIDANCE ON QUESTIONS

1. This question seeks to expose how much we really value God's word when we are suffering. Do we spend time reading it? Do we spend time with Christian brothers and sisters who can help us to understand and remember God's purposes and promises? Do we make it a priority to listen to Bible teaching? In times of crisis, some Christians withdraw from fellowship and Bible teaching. This session challenges us to do the opposite.

2. Paul tells us that the sufferings of Christ flow over into our lives. Paul isn't thinking here about hardships that come our way

because we live in a fallen world (eg: sickness, bereavement, financial loss). Rather, he means hardships that come our way because we are followers of Jesus Christ. This reflects the words of Jesus Himself on a number of occasions eg: Matthew 5 v 10-12, 10 v 34-39; Mark 8 v 31-35; Luke 14 v 26-27; John 15 v 20.

> ☑ **Have you realised that if you are a Christian, you will inevitably suffer the same troubles that Christ suffered?** The only way that these troubles can be avoided is to give up following Christ.

3. If people are familiar with the Gospel accounts of Jesus' life, trial and death, they can share examples of the kinds of things He suffered. Or you could summarise the main events at the end of Jesus' life and get people to make a list of His sufferings. For example: Judas' betrayal, the disciples' desertion, Peter's denial, slanderous accusations, a kangaroo court, mockery and humiliation, gratuitous violence, public execution. This gives us some idea of the sufferings that Christians may also face.

> ☑ **What troubles will you suffer if you don't follow Christ (see Mark 8 v 35-38)?** Those who seek to save their lives from the kind of suffering that Christ met when He took up His cross will lose their lives. Those who respond to people's hostility to Jesus Christ by becoming ashamed of Him will find that when Christ returns, He will reject them.

4. Christians can be confident that they will be comforted in all their troubles by the God of compassion and all comfort. Notice the two uses of 'all'—the 'Father of compassion provides 'all comfort' (v 3) in 'all our troubles' (v 4).

5. v 6: Paul's distress serves the purpose of

bringing comfort and salvation to the Corinthian Christians. Don't assume that Christian suffering will discourage others from the Christian faith. According to Paul, the opposite is true. Christian suffering strengthens our fellow-Christians in their faith, and opens the eyes of non-believers to the Christian good news.

v 9: Paul's testimony is that suffering made him stop relying on himself and made him rely on God instead—a far better outcome since God is the one who 'raises the dead', whereas we have no power to help ourselves or others. In other words, suffering helped Paul keep his own faith on track.

v 11: Paul's suffering spurred other Christians to pray for him. They then had the privilege of seeing God answer their prayers.

• Christians can be content in hardship when they know that their suffering can cause great good in the lives of themselves and others.

6. APPLY: Prepare an example to get the discussion started. People can share about a time when their Christian faith was strengthened after hearing about hardship suffered by fellow-Christians.

7. Paul means that the message of Jesus is brought to the world by people who, according to human standards, appear weak and even at times defeated. Many imagine that a message about 'the glory of Christ, who is the image of God' (v 4) would come to our world through great men of military might, a mass movement of multitudes, huge political influence and wealth etc. Instead, the Christian message came through a small group of despised men who, without any wealth, influence or trappings of power, travelled around and simply spoke to people. Often they

met with hostility, persecution, and suffering. If people in your group are new to the Bible, encourage them to read the story of how the church first grew in the New Testament book of Acts.

8. God wants people to know that the power of the gospel comes from God, not from men (v 7). When Christians are 'given over to death for Jesus' sake' (ie: they suffer persecution for following Christ), Jesus' life is also revealed in them (v 10-11). In other words, when Christians suffer hardship, and yet continue in love, forgiveness, peace, hope and joy because of Jesus, others will see God's supernatural power at work and some will turn to the gospel.

9. APPLY: Imagine how a Christian might suffer for their faith (preferably an example that is relevant to your group), and get people to work out how the power of God could be displayed in this situation. Eg: A young person is thrown out of home when they become a Christian, and cut off from their family; an employee is sidelined and unable to progress in their career, because their boss hates Christians; in a country where Christians are a minority, church premises are fire-bombed and permission to rebuild is refused; a street-preacher is unjustly charged with hate-crime and ends up in prison.

10. Paul continues to preach the gospel through hardship because he knows that this is how God's grace reaches people, and he looks forward to the day when he will stand in the presence of God alongside those who heard the gospel from him.

• Paul looks forward to eternal glory that will far outweigh all his troubles now. In comparison with eternal glory, Paul describes all his troubles as 'light and momentary'. This is an amazing statement when we consider what Paul actually went through during his life (see 11 v 23-29).

• If eternal glory will far outweigh all our troubles, then our hardships now must be worth suffering. Also, we needn't feel that our hardships are causing us to miss out in any way, since we will be unimaginably compensated in the future for everything we have suffered now. It is vital to know truths like this before hardships come our way. In the midst of suffering, people may be too overwhelmed with pain to listen to and accept Paul's words here—we need to be ready ahead of time.

Note: This truth also has important application for what we expect from life now. Many people pursue experiences now, like foreign travel etc—50 things to do before you die! Believers will be set free from this, understanding that eternity will give us all these things and more. We are set free to pursue gospel goals.

11. APPLY: In this session we have seen how Paul understood what God was doing through the hardships that he suffered. Paul also trusted that God would fulfil what He had promised in the future—eternal glory. Paul's experiences and understanding are found in God's word, and are there for our benefit. We can share his contentment (and even joy) in hardship as we rely on the same promises and revelation about God that Paul relied on. Discuss practical ideas about how we can saturate our minds with God's word, so that when suffering comes our way, we will remember and live by these things, as Paul did.

EXPLORE MORE: Philippians 4 v 4-13
• Paul is able to rejoice in suffering (v 4, 10) and he has peace from God 'which transcends all understanding' (v 7).
• He can feel like this because…
v 6-7: he prays to God about everything;

v 8: he keeps his mind focused on God's Word, not on the lies of the world;
v 10: he stays in contact with God's people and enjoys his fellowship with them.

• Our refuge in suffering is our relationship with God through our Lord Jesus Christ. It is by turning to Him, listening to Him, trusting Him, and living for His plans and purposes that we can not only survive hardships but be content, joyful and at peace.

• Paul has learned the secret of being content in any situation. The fact that he has learned this shows that contentment doesn't come naturally—it takes time and effort to discover how we can be content. But also, because it is not a matter of the right circumstances or personality, anyone can become content if they are willing to learn from God.

• The secret of Paul's contentment is his reliance on God for strength (v 13). As we saw in question 4, it is in the midst of troubles that we learn to rely on 'the God of all comfort, who comforts us in all our troubles' (2 Corinthians 1 v 3-4). Then, when we rely on God for strength, we can do everything, including being content in every situation, even suffering.

OPTIONAL EXTRA

(As a prelude to prayer) Use the internet to look up current news items about the persecuted church. Useful organisations include:
• Voice of the Martyrs www.persecution.com
• Barnabas Fund www.barnabasfund.org
• Open Doors International. www.od.org

Share stories of Christians facing hardships in countries such as Iraq or North Korea. If appropriate, you could ask someone in your group to do this.

Luke 6 v 12-26

THE SECRET OF TRUE HAPPINESS

THE BIG IDEA

Jesus followers will only be truly happy when they experience poverty, hunger and grief as the Spirit opens their eyes to our need for Jesus Christ, and when we are hated, excluded, insulted and slandered for following Him.

SUMMARY

In this final session, we return to the words of Jesus Himself as He gives His disciples the secret of true happiness in our fallen world. In this passage, Jesus is speaking to the Twelve—those that He has just chosen to take His good news to the whole world. This marks the beginning of the church, and what Jesus says here will be the pattern for all those who follow Him.

Although the passage doesn't mention contentment, Jesus' repeated assertion that those who live as His disciples are 'blessed' is clearly relevant to the issue of contentment. It is striking that Jesus promises blessedness (true happiness) from a life which seems to offer precisely the opposite. 'Blessed' describes the true position of Jesus' disciples now that He is their Lord, rather than the feelings of His disciples in the various situations mentioned (poverty, hunger, weeping, an object of hatred, excluded, insulted and slandered). However, by understanding our true position we can also feel joy—Jesus tells His disciples to 'leap for joy' because of what awaits them (v 23).

The session looks at what it means to be

poor, to hunger and weep now, to be hated, excluded, insulted and rejected as evil because of the Son of Man, as well as what it means to be 'blessed'. Questions 5-7 tie in with previous sessions and give people an opportunity to revise the whole course. People are challenged to test whether they really believe Jesus' words. Is the kind of life described here by Jesus what we really want most for our children? Will we resist the temptation to envy non-believers when we understand their final destiny? On a practical level, there is an opportunity to consider how we can talk to non-Christians about true happiness, and to think about the way that our joy in Christ can be expressed and shown to others, both as individuals and as a church.

GUIDANCE ON QUESTIONS

1. This question reveals what people find most important in life. People are prepared to put up with all sorts of unsatisfactory things themselves that they would not want their children to experience. We shall see from this passage that Jesus promises blessedness, or true happiness, from a life which seems to offer precisely the opposite. The question for us is: Do we trust what Jesus says or do we prefer to follow our own recipe for happiness?

2. The word 'blessed' means 'happy'. The word 'woe' means 'bitter grief' or distress.

3. See table opposite.

Luke 6	What do other verses tell us?	What does Jesus mean in Luke 6?
Poor (v 20)	Matthew 5 v 3: Poor in spirit Luke 7 v 21-22: Jesus preached the good news to the poor.	The poor are those who have nothing to offer God and no way of paying for their sin. They need to be rescued by someone who can pay for their sin. This is the good news that Jesus preached. (See 2 Corinthians 8 v 9.)
Hungry (v 21)	Matthew 5 v 6: Those who hunger and thirst for righteousness John 6 v 35: Jesus told people to believe in Him, the bread of life.	The hungry are those who know they are not right with God, and that they cannot become righteous by themselves. They need someone to make them righteous. God, in His grace, gives righteousness to those who believe in Jesus. (See Philippians 3 v 8-9.)
Weeping (v 21)	Luke 7 v 36-39: Jesus commended the weeping woman because she came to Jesus, trusting Him for the forgiveness of her many sins.	People who weep and mourn are those whose sin, and inability to overcome sin, makes them 'weep'. God is pleased with weeping when it causes us to turn to Jesus. (See Romans 7 v 21-25a.)

4. Jesus promises His disciples that they are part of the kingdom of God, that their hunger for righteousness (their need to be right with God) will be satisfied, and their grief at sin will be replaced with joy. Poverty, hunger and weeping are only half of the story. But more than that, they are visible signs of the invisible blessings that Jesus promises.

• v 20b—'yours is the kingdom of heaven'. Through the good news of Jesus Christ, God has done what 'poor' people cannot do—He has brought them into His kingdom. Jesus' statement to those who are poor is in the present tense. Although we look forward to a day when we will be completely free our poverty, hunger and grief, we are also blessed now in our poverty, hunger and grief, by being part of God's kingdom—we are under His protection and guidance, and enjoy all the privileges of being His subjects.

Note: the kingdom of God/heaven = the community of all those throughout history and worldwide who recognise God as king, and submit to His rule in their lives = all those who believe in Jesus.

5. Jesus expects that people will hate His disciples, exclude them, insult them and reject them as evil. The reason for this is because of Jesus—who He is and what He has done. People reject Jesus (and therefore persecute His disciples) because their deeds are evil (John 3 v 19-20). We may be hated for all sorts of reasons—our personality, politics, ethnic origin, or because of someone's envy. But if we are disciples of Jesus, in addition to these reasons, we will also be hated for our love for and commitment to Jesus.

6. Given the situation that Jesus is describing here, His words 'Rejoice in that day and leap for joy' are striking. First get people to share situations in which they have literally leapt for joy. Eg: passing exams, getting a job, accepting a marriage proposal, finding out you are pregnant etc. Then move on to talk about this kind of joy when you are suffering for your faith.

• The kind of joy that Jesus promises does not come from our circumstances but from our faith. Some in the group may not be able to imagine that they could rejoice when they are facing hardship. Point them to Acts 16 v 22-25; Hebrews 10 v 34.

7. In the future, Jesus talks about 'that day'. His disciples can rejoice now in a day that is coming and will reveal their great reward in heaven ie: the day when Jesus returns to this earth to take His disciples to be with Him forever (see 1 Thess 4 v 13-17).

We are to **look back** to the prophets—and also other Christians in the past—who were persecuted. If our experience is their experience, then we can rejoice that we are on the right lines!

8. APPLY: This question gives your group an opportunity to summarise not only this session but the whole course, and for Christians to think about how they can talk about these things with others. The answer is a resounding 'yes', but we need to think about how most people understand 'happiness', how and why Jesus gives us a different kind of happiness, and the fact that in this world Christians are blessed now, and yet are still waiting for perfect happiness.You could divide people into pairs and get them to practise or write down a one-minute answer to this question based on everything they have learned so far.

9. APPLY: As Christians, the thing that we should want most for the children in our lives is that they become disciples of Jesus

Christ; that they experience poverty, hunger and grief as the Spirit opens their eyes to their need for Jesus; that they turn to Jesus Christ as their Lord and Saviour, and live a life of being hated, excluded, insulted and slandered for Him. If we find it hard to want this for our children, do we really trust Jesus when He says that people who live like this are 'blessed' ie: happy?

10. We should constantly remind ourselves of the future that awaits those who reject Jesus Christ (John 3 v 18). Now is as good as it gets, none of the fun and enjoyment will last, and their future is summed up in the word 'Woe'!

Explore More: Psalm 23
• The psalm promises that when the Lord is our shepherd, everything that we need will be provided—we will not be in want.
• David, the writer, mentions walking through the valley of the shadow of death (v 4) and being in the presence of his enemies (v 5)—clearly, he is thinking of very difficult and dangerous situations.
• David can be content in difficult, dangerous situations—he fears no evil and is comforted (v 4) because the Lord is with him, just as Jesus' disciples can be blessed when they are hated, excluded, insulted and rejected for following Christ.
• The key to David's contentment in all situations is the fact that the Lord is His shepherd (v 1). Again, we see that it is our right relationship with the Lord that brings contentment.
• A shepherd cares for, guides and protects his sheep, and knows each one of his sheep personally and intimately (see John 10 v 10-16). Through Jesus, we can receive the same kind of care from God that this sheep receives from the shepherd.

11. APPLY: This question allows people to

think about how (or whether) joy is expressed when we meet together with other Christians at church. Don't limit the discussion to formal expressions of joy eg: singing in the meetings. What about our prayers? What about our conversations with others after Bible teaching, and over refreshments? What about opportunities for sharing answers to prayer, wonderful things learned from God's Word, testimonies (stories) of how people have become Christians or grown in faith, etc?

• If joy seems lacking in church, here are some questions to think about:
Are we living in the light of the gospel, or do our lives simply reflect the desires and limited understanding of the non-believing world around us?

Are we reminding ourselves and each other of 'real reality'?

Are we praying for the power of the Holy Spirit in our lives, or just following rules and traditions?

Note: We must remember that people have different characters, and those who are shyer or more reserved should not be press-ganged into exuberant displays of joy that are foreign to their nature. But each of us will have an individual way of expressing joy. Are we showing others, Christians and non-Christians, that we are full of joy?

OPTIONAL EXTRA
(As an introduction to the idea that Jesus' secret of true happiness is counter-intuitive.) Tell the famous story (probably a myth) about the polar explorer Ernest Shackleton, who was supposed to have written the following advertisement for volunteers to man an expedition to the Antarctic.

Men wanted for hazardous journey. Low wages, bitter cold, long hours of complete darkness. Safe return doubtful. Honour and recognition in event of success.

Divide people into pairs or small groups and get them to invent a similar advertisement for a job that stresses all the difficulties and disadvantages. Later in the session (eg: question 4) you can discuss how Jesus' words in Luke 6 are similar to or different from Shackleton's advertisement, and those of your group (Jesus promises blessing now and His promises are sure).

Demolishing Discontent

If you think that your group would be interested in some further reflection during the week, there is a 'homework' option, available as a free download from the Good Book Company website called *Demolishing Discontent*. This aims to help Christians discover biblical antidotes to discontent—fear of the Lord, trust, hope, love, service and mission. Each week there are several Bible passages to read and some questions to think about, often involving a practical 'project' that people can undertake to help themselves grow in Christian contentment. Visit the Good Book Company website and find it as a download on the page for this book, or in the downloads section:

www.thegoodbook.co.uk/downloads

At The Good Book Company, we are dedicated to helping Christians and local churches grow. We believe that God's growth process always starts with hearing clearly what He has said to us through His timeless word—the Bible.

Ever since we opened our doors in 1991, we have been striving to produce resources that honour God in the way the Bible is used. We have grown to become an international provider of user-friendly resources to the Christian community, with believers of all backgrounds and denominations using our Bible studies, books, evangelistic resources, DVD-based courses and training events.

We want to equip ordinary Christians to live for Christ day by day, and churches to grow in their knowledge of God, their love for one another, and the effectiveness of their outreach. Call us to discuss your needs, or visit **www.thegoodbook.co.uk**, for more information on the resources and services we provide.

 www.thegoodbook.co.uk
admin@thegoodbook.co.uk

 0845 225 0880

 Elm House,
37 Elm Road,
New Malden, Surrey
KT3 3HB, UK

Also available in the Good Book Guide series...

Psalms: Soul Songs
6 studies. ISBN: 9781904889960

David: God's True King
6 studies. ISBN: 9781904889984

Ezekiel: The God of Glory
6 studies. ISBN: 9781904889274

Zechariah: God's Big Plan
6 studies. ISBN: 9781904889267

Mark 1-8: The Coming King
10 studies. ISBN: 9781904889281

Mark 9-16: The Servant King
7 studies. ISBN: 9781904889519

Romans 1-5: God and You
6 studies. ISBN: 9781904889618

1 Thessalonians: Living to please God
7 studies. ISBN: 9781904889533

2 Timothy: Faithful to the end
7 studies. ISBN: 9781905564569

1 Peter: Living in the real world
5 studies. ISBN: 9781904889496

1 John: How to be sure
7 studies. ISBN: 9781904889953

Revelation 2-3: A message from Jesus to the church today
7 studies. ISBN: 9781905564682

TOPICAL STUDIES
- **Biblical Womanhood** 9 studies.
- **Women of Faith from the OT** 8 studies.
- **Meeting Jesus: NT women of faith** 8 studies.
- **The Holy Spirit** 8 studies.
- **Man of God** 10 studies.
- **The Apostles Creed** 10 studies.
- **Work Songs** 6 studies.

Visit www.thegoodbook.co.uk to order or call us on 0845 225 0880 for further details